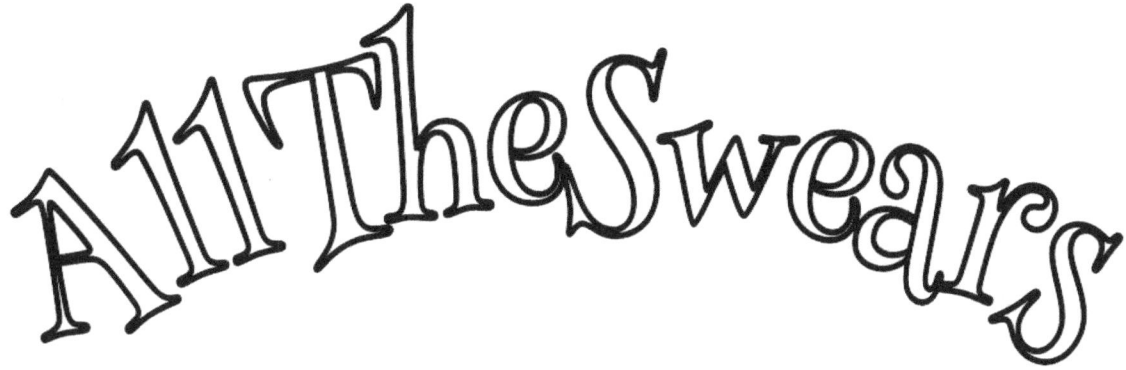

All The Swears

An Irreverent and Fucking Awesome Coloring Book
For Adults Who Just Need
Time To Fucking Chill and
Find Their Zen

BY

SCARLET HAYES
OF
DOWN THE HOLE

&

AMBER LITE
OF
MOMMY NEEDS WINE, NOT WHINE

*Note: This book is not for the easily butt hurt wankers who get sand in their mimsies by the dumpster load. If the previous sentence describes you, then you might want to go find a coloring book with baby animals, mandalas, or shit like that.

Madcasm Publishing, LLC
P.O. Box 686
Delaware, Ohio 43015
dthscarlet@gmail.com
www.madcasm.com

Limits of Liability and Disclaimer of Warranty
The authors and publisher shall not be liable for your misuse of this material. This book is for entertainment purposes only and is intended for adult audiences only.

Warning & Disclaimer
The purpose of this book is to entertain the reader/colorer/artist/person who picked up this book and thought, "Hey, I want to color some inappropriate animals and sweary words. Why the hell not?" The authors and/or publisher do not guarantee that anyone using any information contained within this book will become smarter, successful, get laid, become more creative, or learn how to become as talented as the authors and/or publisher by osmosis or any other means. The authors and/or publisher shall have neither liability nor responsibility with respect to any loss or damage caused, or alleged to be caused, directly or indirectly, by the information contained within this book. In other words, don't be a fucking numb nuts and leave this book out in your cubicle and then try to blame us when your uptight twat of a boss fires you because you were coloring a peniscock during work hours. Or when the alter boys catch you coloring a llama with a ballgag during confession. Just don't. We have good lawyers and we are telling you now – don't be a twat licking cunt monkey and try to sue us because you make bad choices. This is an ADULT coloring book for irreverent, smart-assed, good (or ill) humored people over the age of consent.

So, as Frankie said, "Relax." And as we say, "Grab a glass of wine (or bourbon or beer or whatever the fuck you want to drink – capri sun if that's your thing), park your ass in your favorite comfy spot, chill the fuck out, and get your coloring zen on."

Peace, love, and zero fucks given for anything politically correct or appropriate.

XOXO,
Scarlet and Amber

Dedications

First and foremost, we would like to dedicate this book to you, the people willing to pick up this book and take a chance on two crazy friends who came up with one of about a thousand ideas and decided that this was the one we were going to make stick first.

May you find this book as enjoyable to work through, read, color, and talk about as we did creating it.

Special Dedications From Scarlet

This project would not have been possible if it were not for the support of my incredibly supportive and equally twisted partner in crime, my husband, Ace. As the great e.e. cummings so aptly described, I carry his heart in my heart.

My children, Slim and Bat Squirrel. They are the lights of my life. My sun and my moon. And they are also the genesis of many of the epithets that you will find contained within the volumes of AllTheSwears because lets face it, kids can bring out the best in us and also make us contemplate running away more as adults than we ever did as children.

I would like to thank my crazy tribe of Mad Hatters from my blog, Down The Hole, where you can find me swearing on the regular at facebook.com/downthehole. I'm pretty sure that without this group of ever-growing friends and like-minded weirdos, I never would have undertaken this project.

And finally, the She to my Nanigans, my co-author and partner in crime, Amber. Woman, we've run the gamut of craziness in the few short years we've known each other, but when you can look at someone and say "platypussy" and ten minutes later have a sketch in your inbox exactly how you envisioned it, you know you've found your person. Thanks for being as weird as me.

Special Dedications from Amber

I dedicate this awesomely inappropriate adventure to a few very important people in my life.

First, to my dad. I am pretty sure if it were not for him, I never would have become the creative genius that I think I am, today. He is my rock and sometimes he is the rock that knocks me in the head when I float just a bit too far away from reality.

I also dedicate this to my daughter, the roots and acorn of my twisted tree. She is the ultimate creation I could ever have made and every day, I look at her and couldn't be more amazed at the masterpiece that she has become and continues to develop into every single day. I love you, baby girl.

Also, Scarlet, thanks for kicking my ass and getting me back into the groove. The Shenanigirls are alive and well, and this shit fucking rocks.

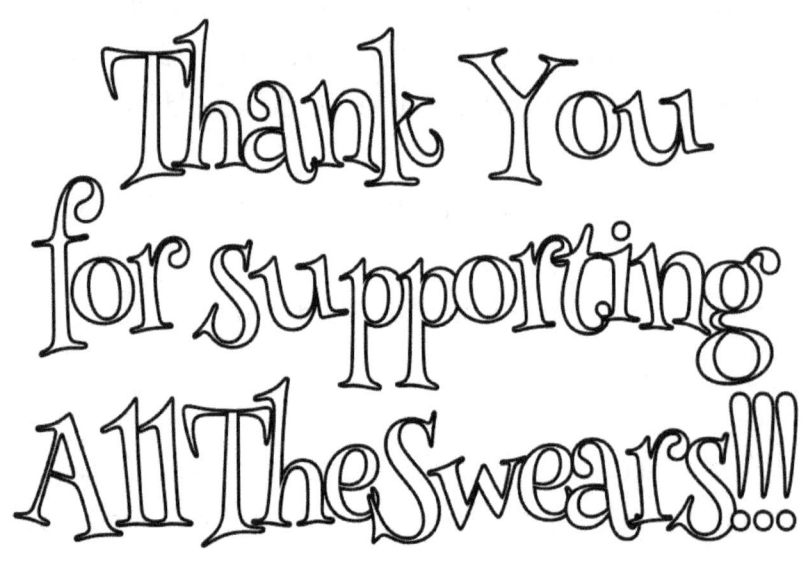

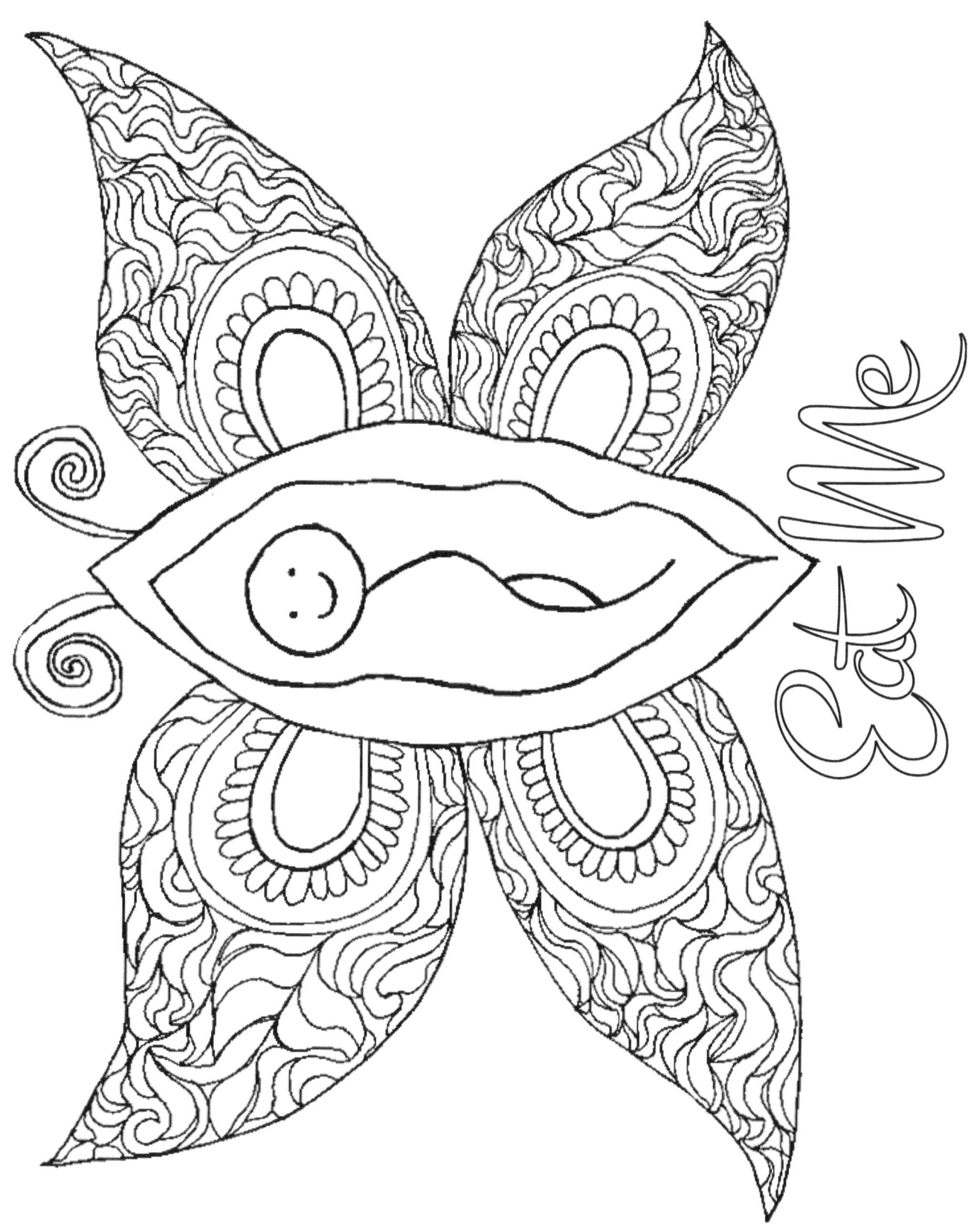

Eat Me

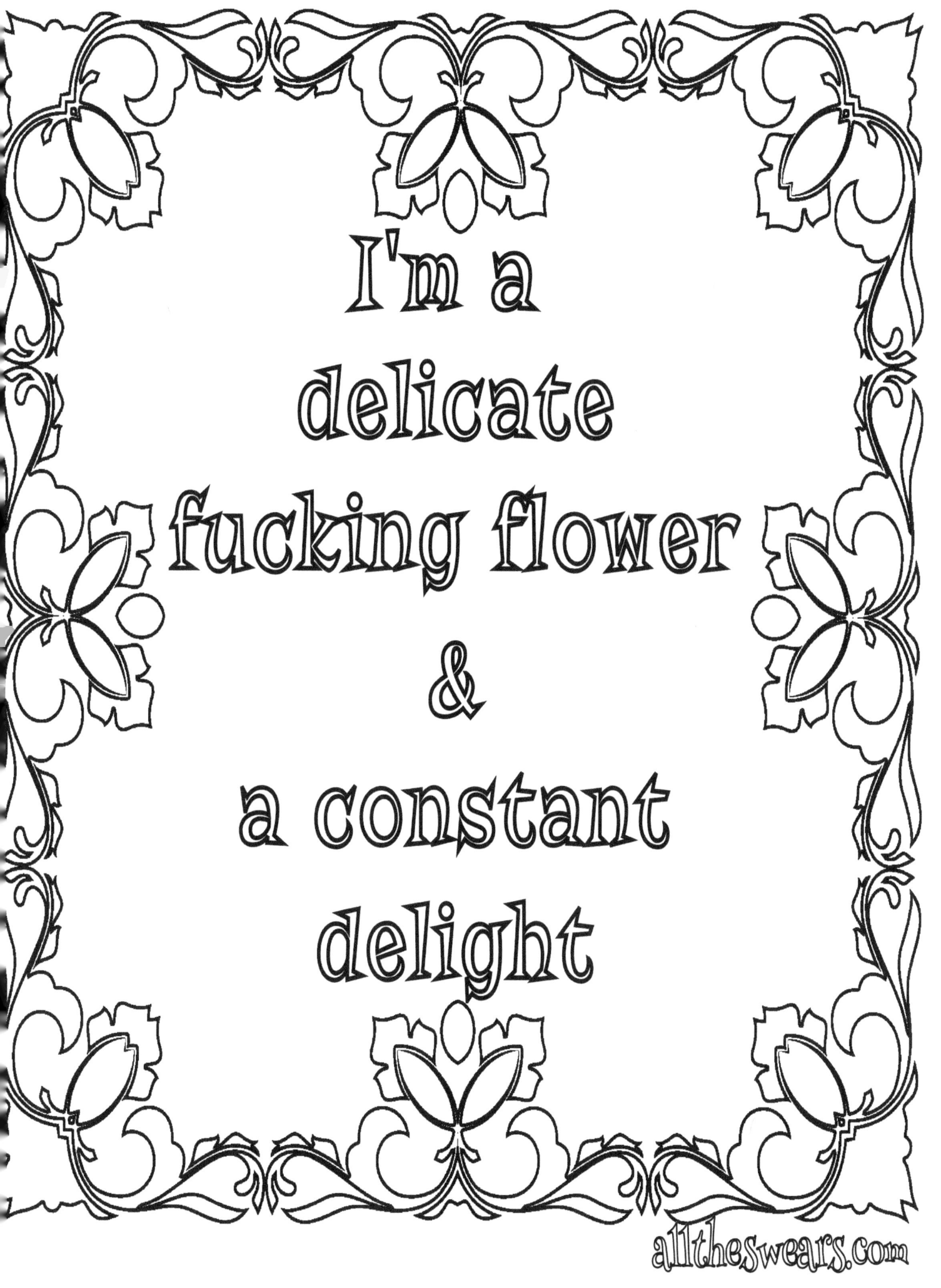

I'm a delicate fucking flower & a constant delight

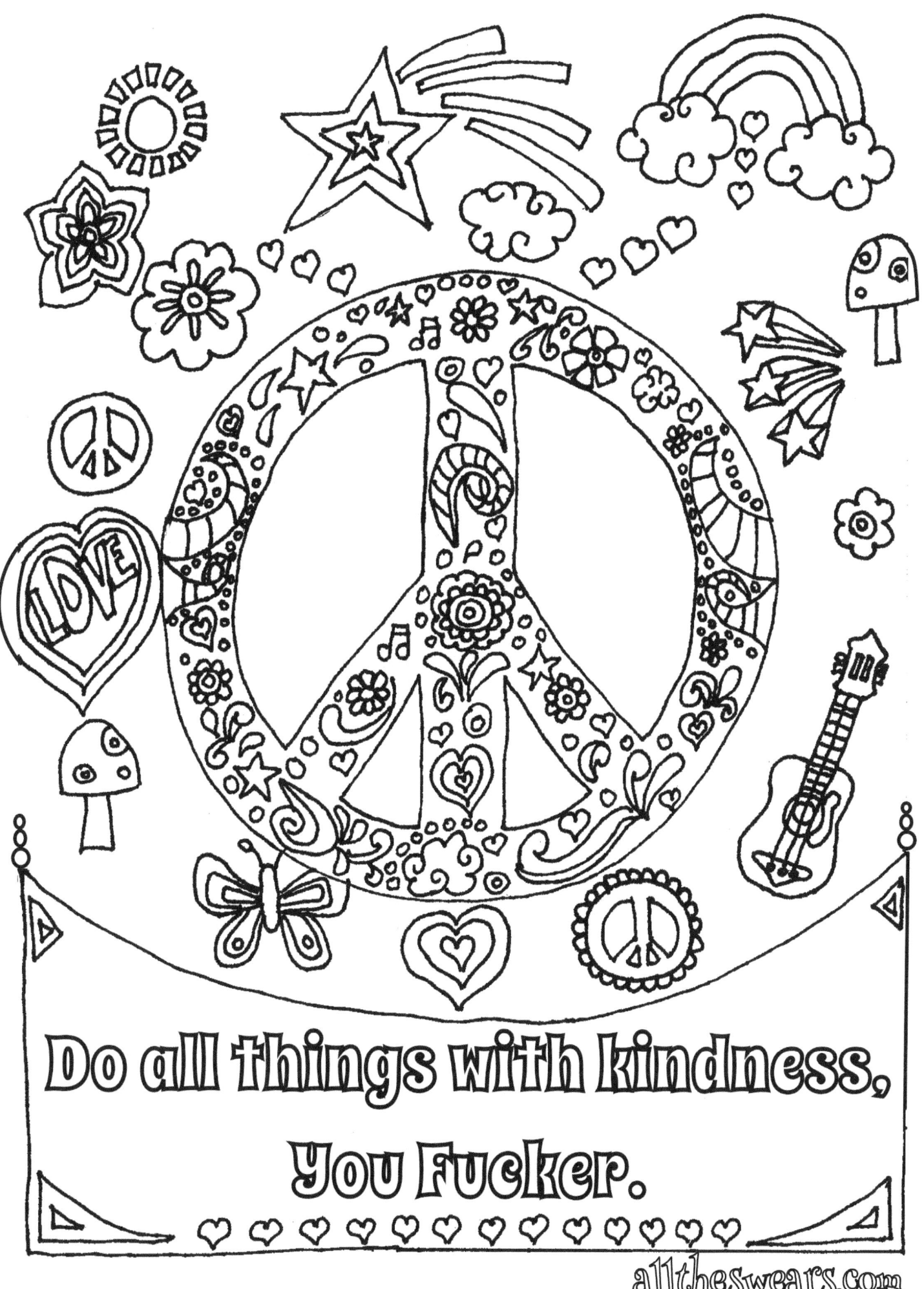

Do all things with kindness,

You Fucker.

alltheswears.com

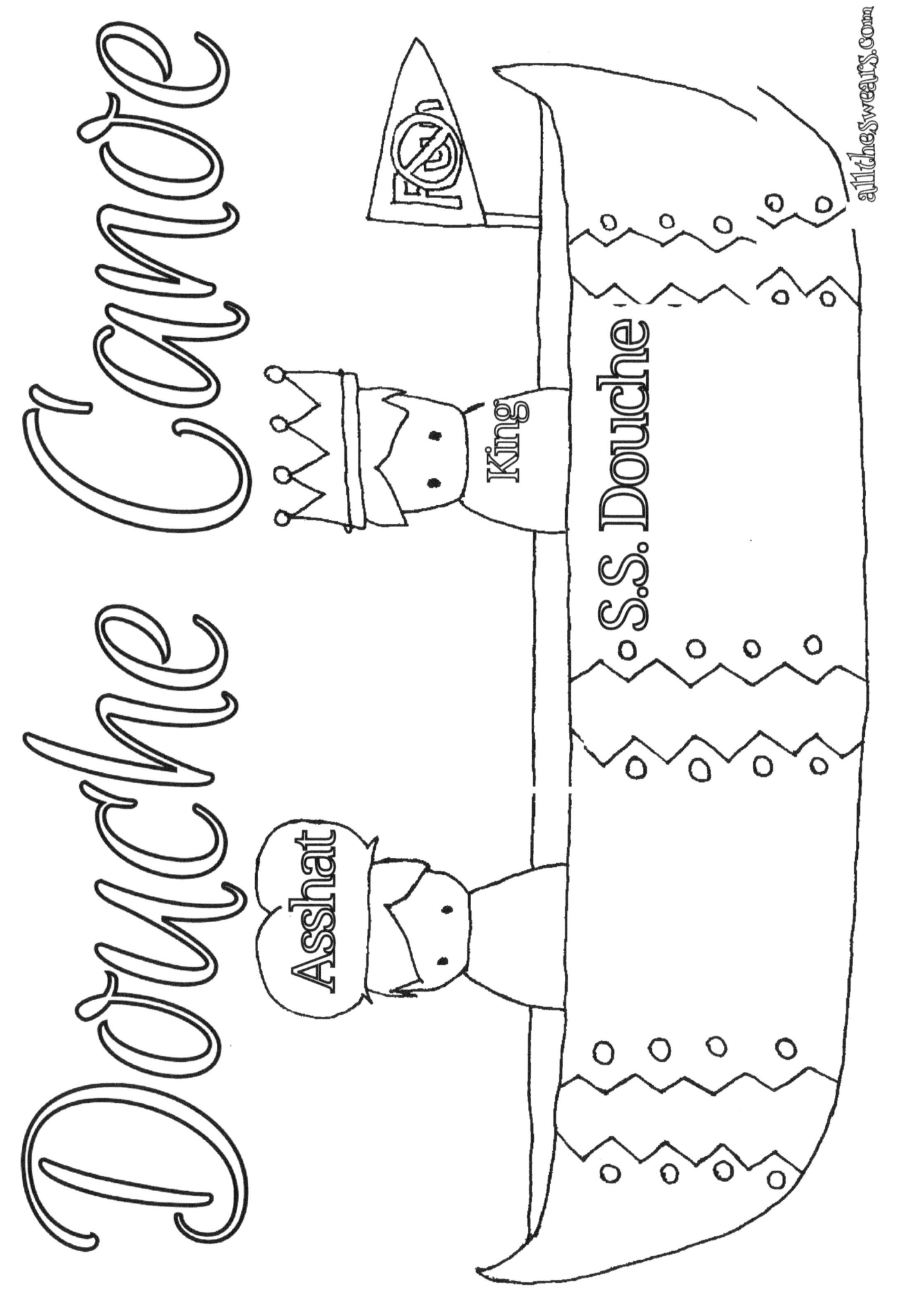

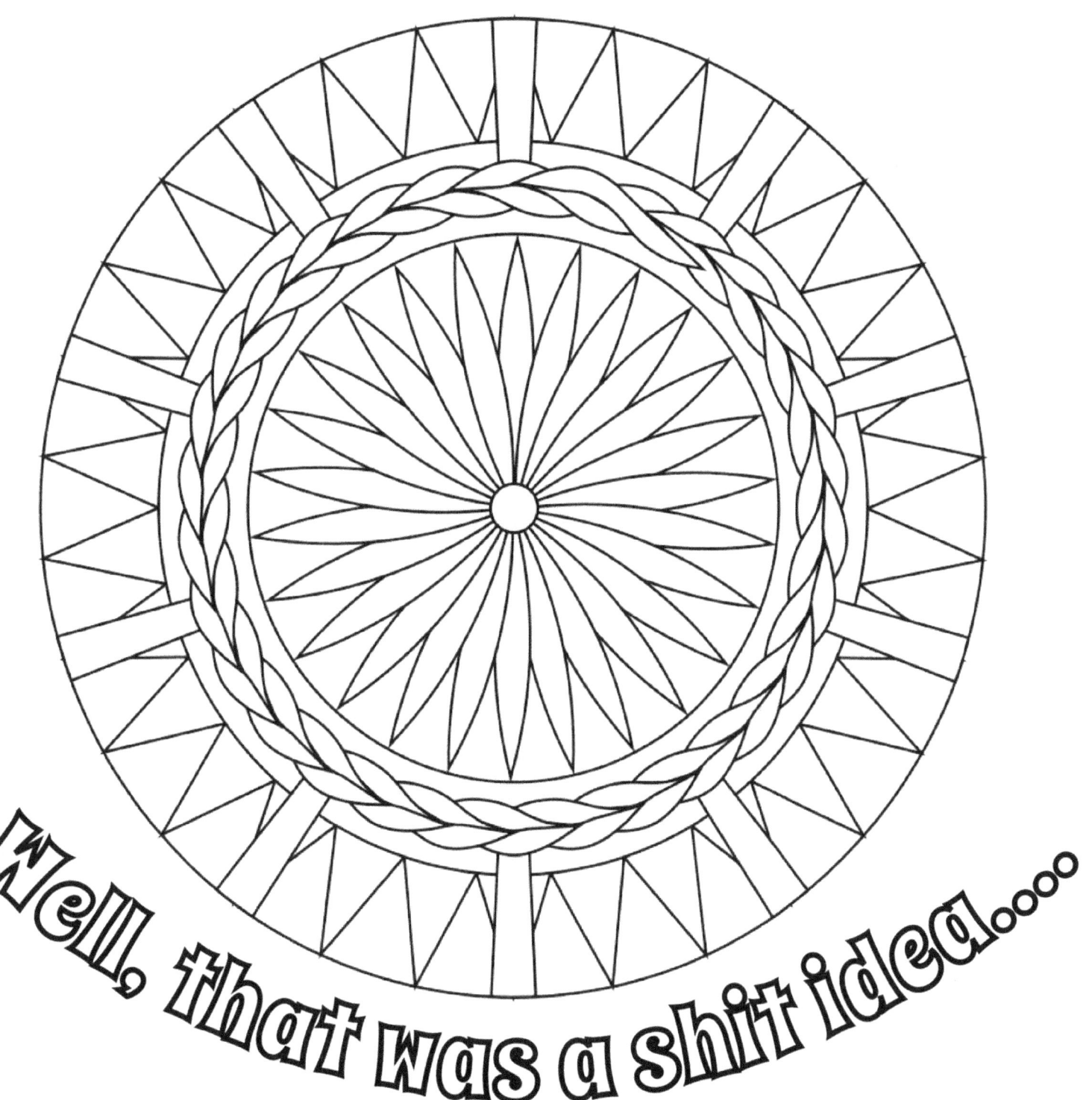

Well, that was a shit idea....

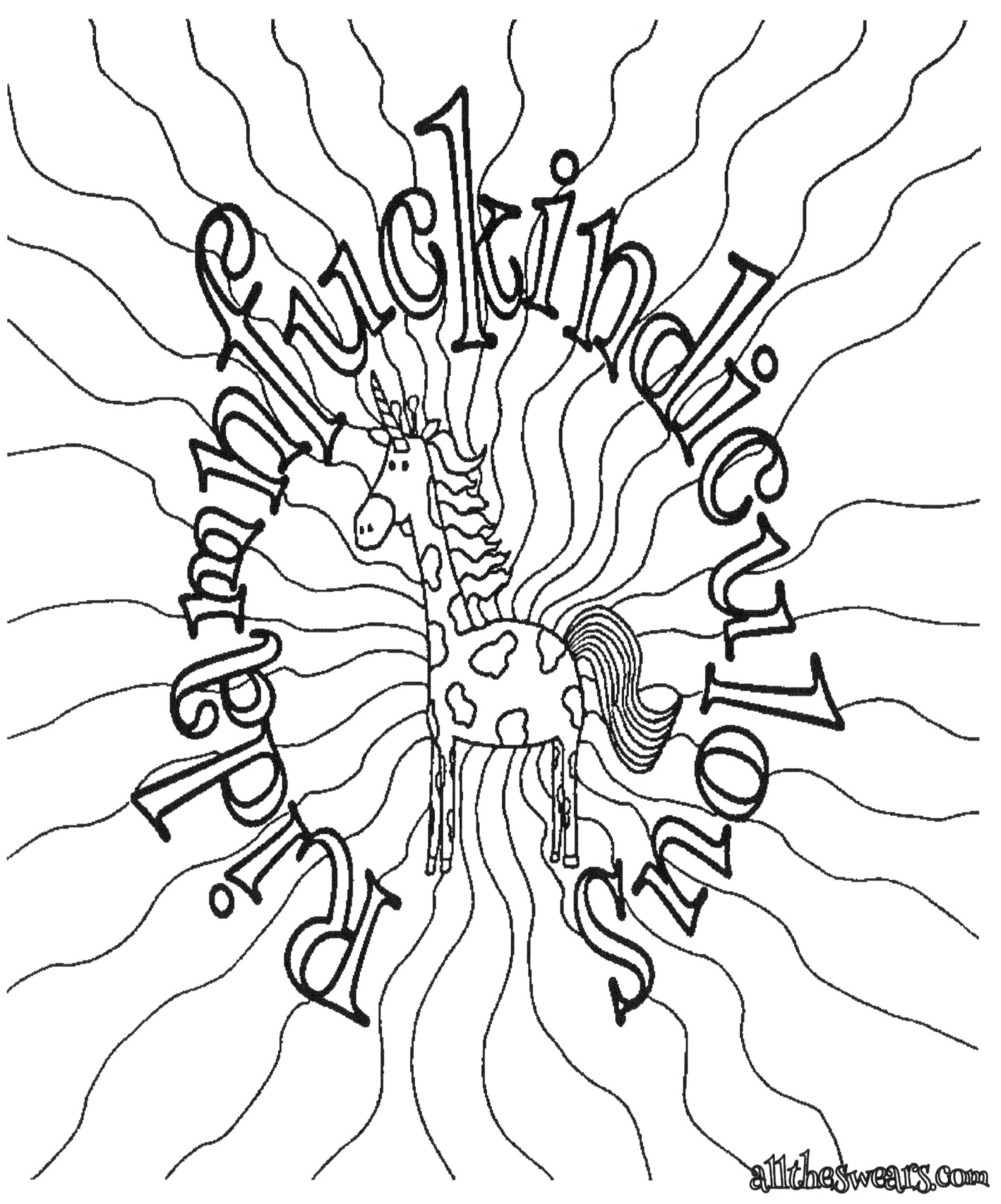

ridiculkindiculous

allthesweats.com

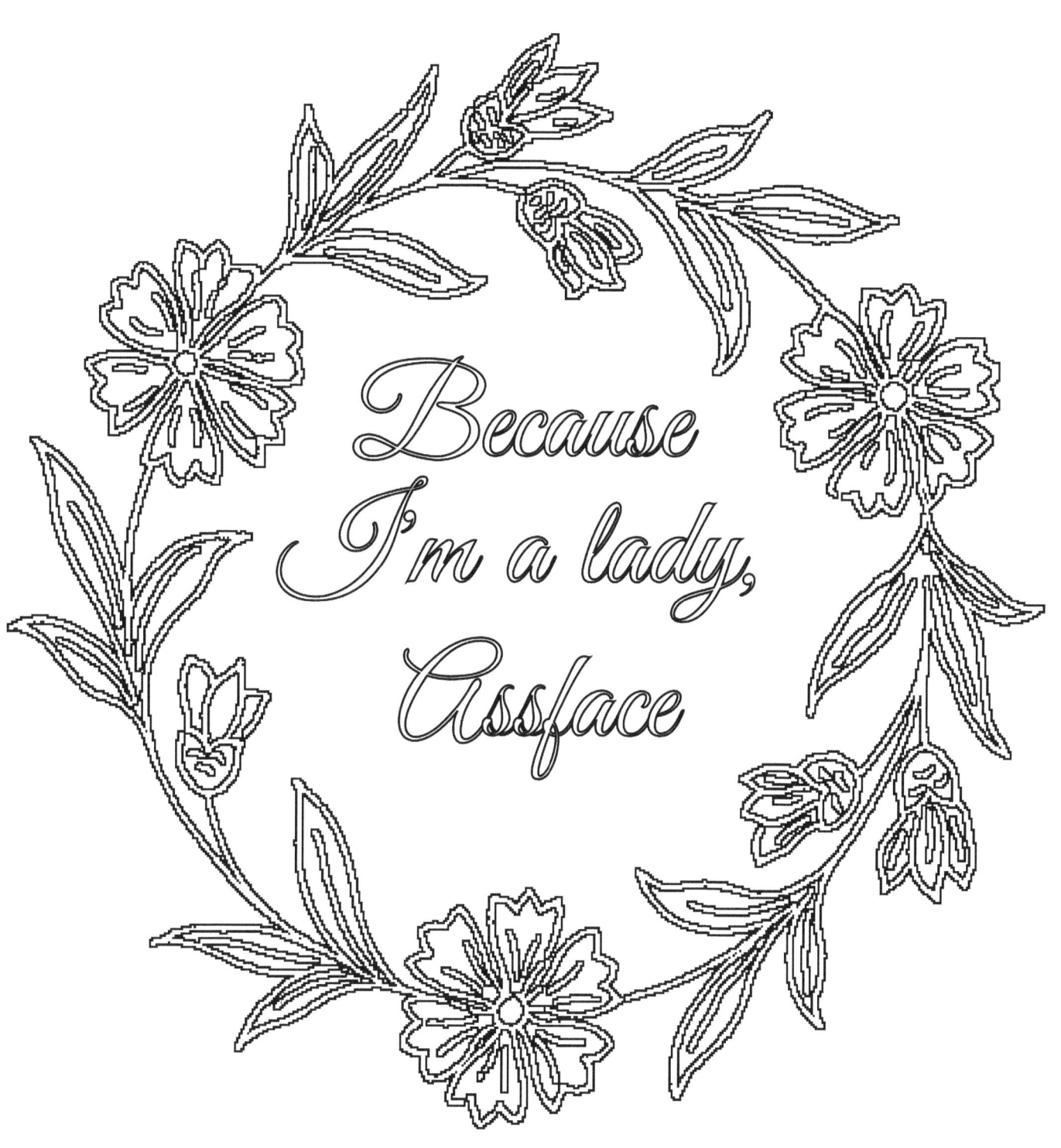

Because I'm a lady, Assface

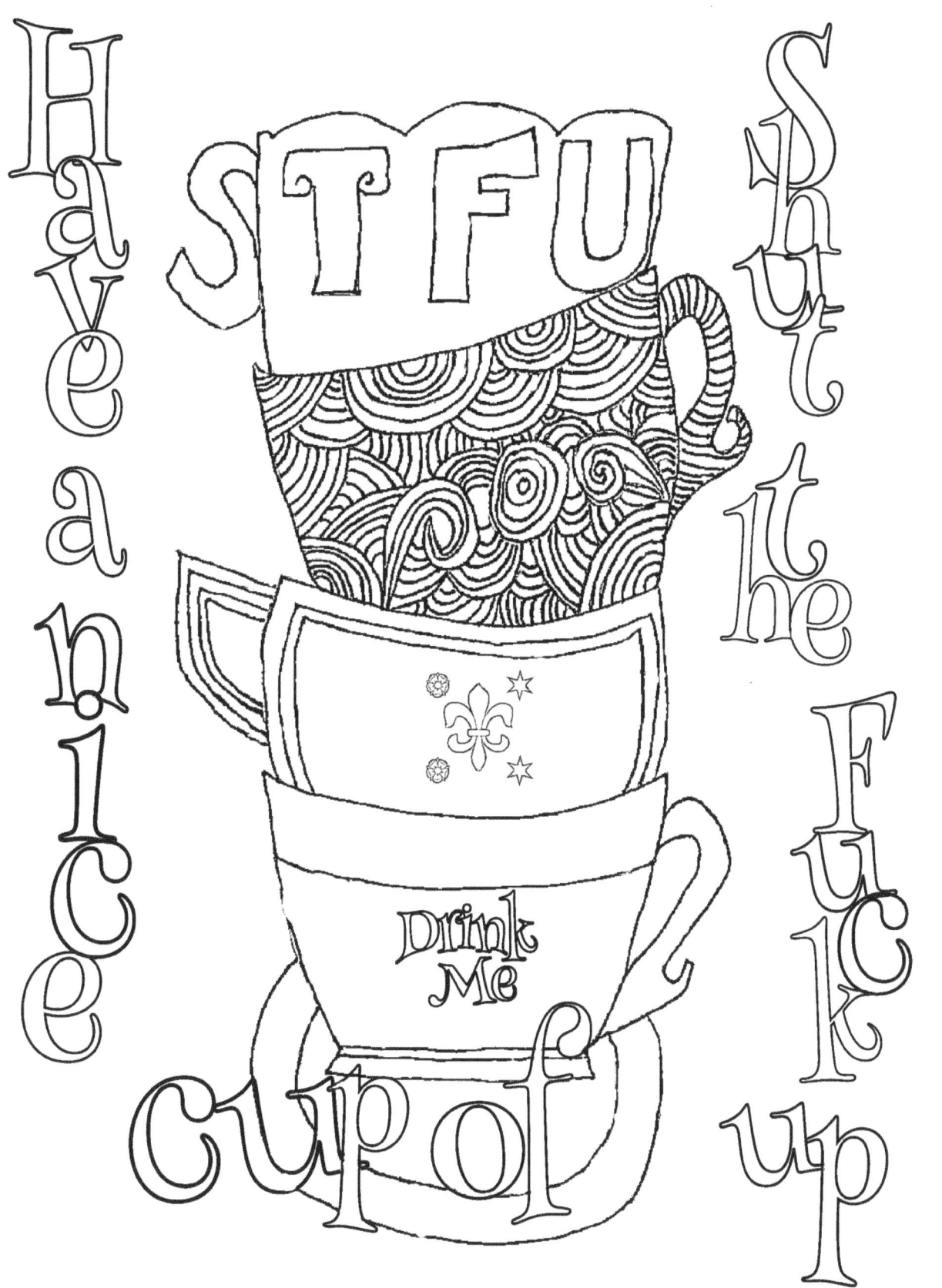

Have a nice Cup of

STFU

Shut the Fuck up

Drink Me

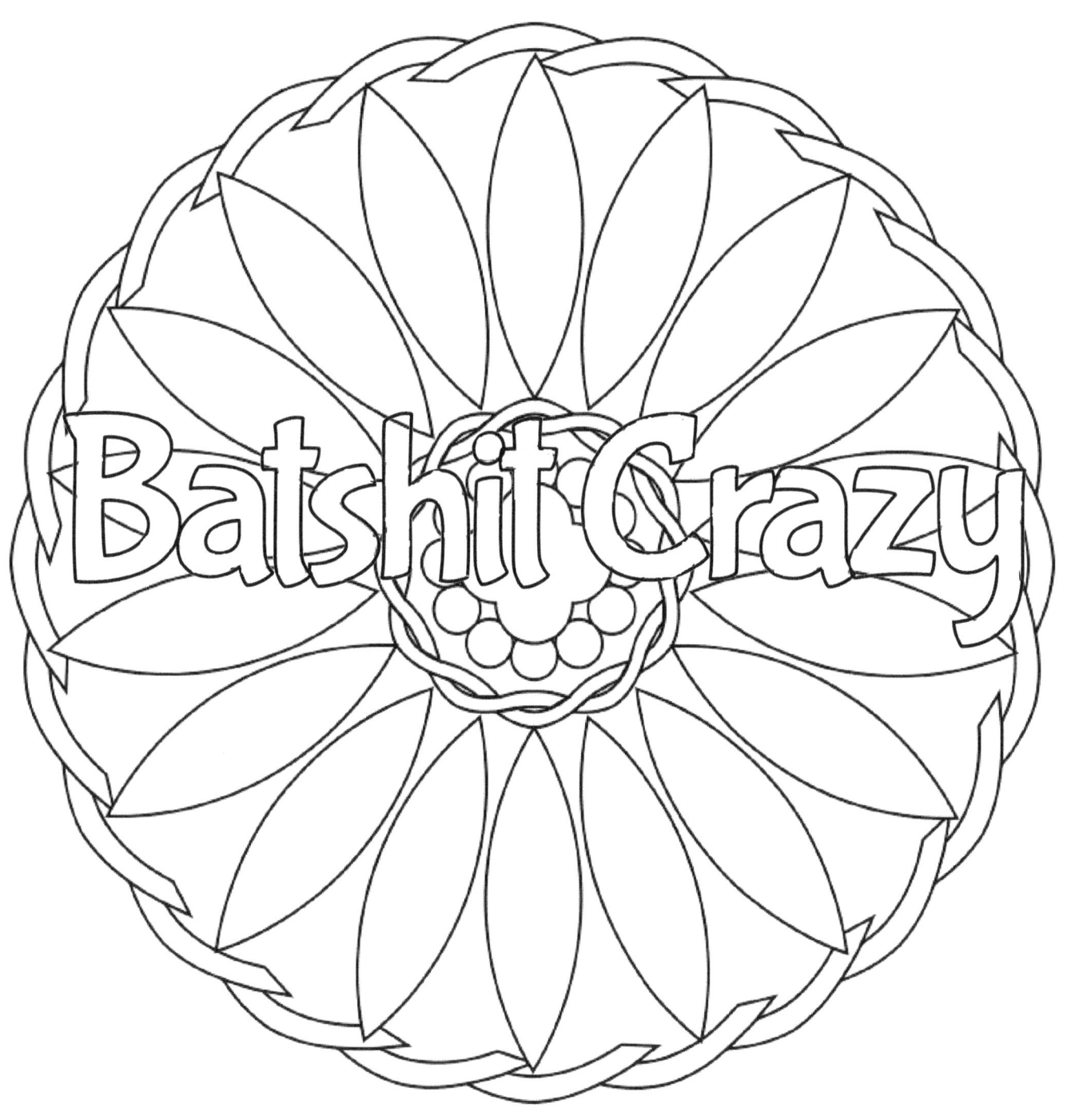

allthes웨ars.com

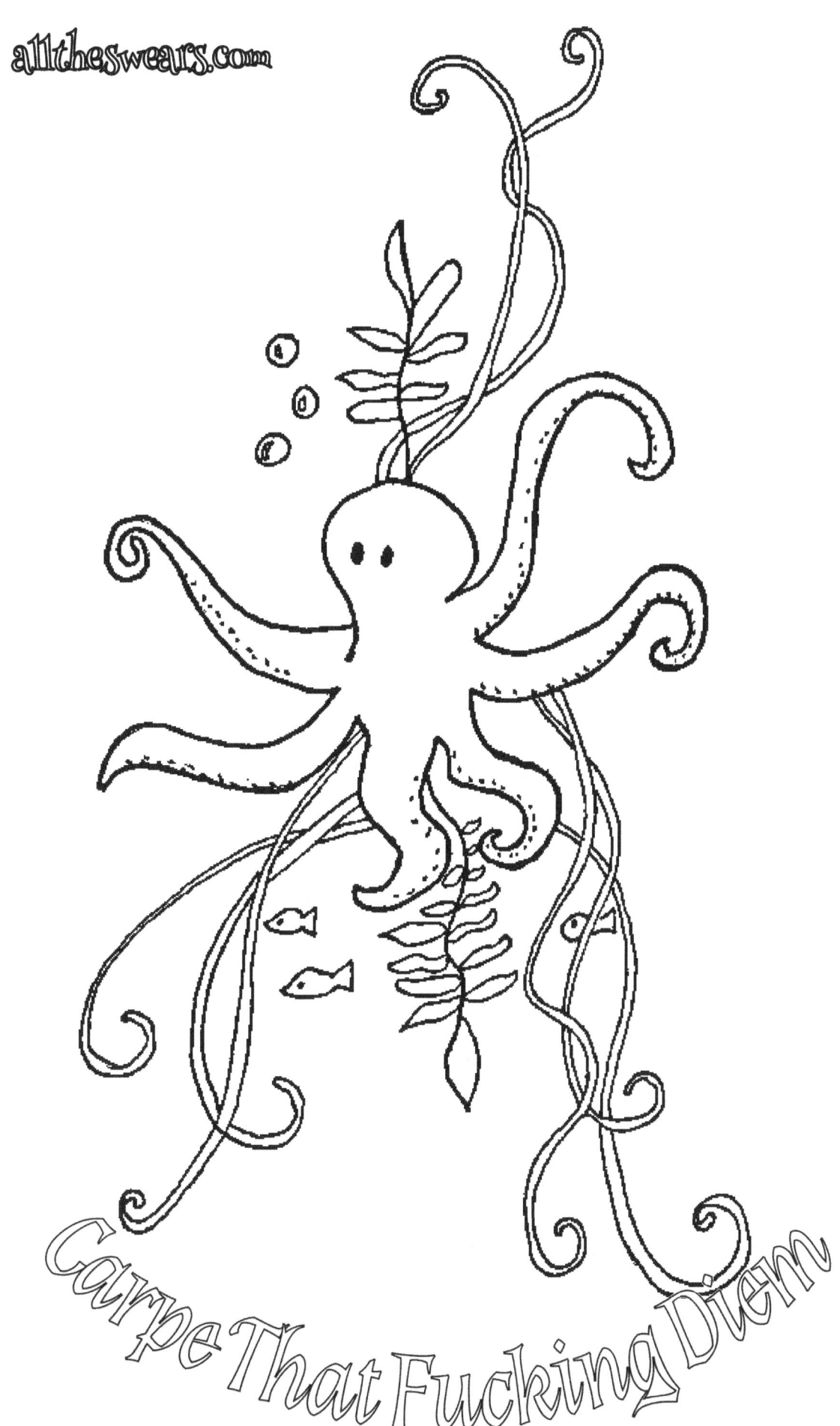

Carpe That Fucking Diem

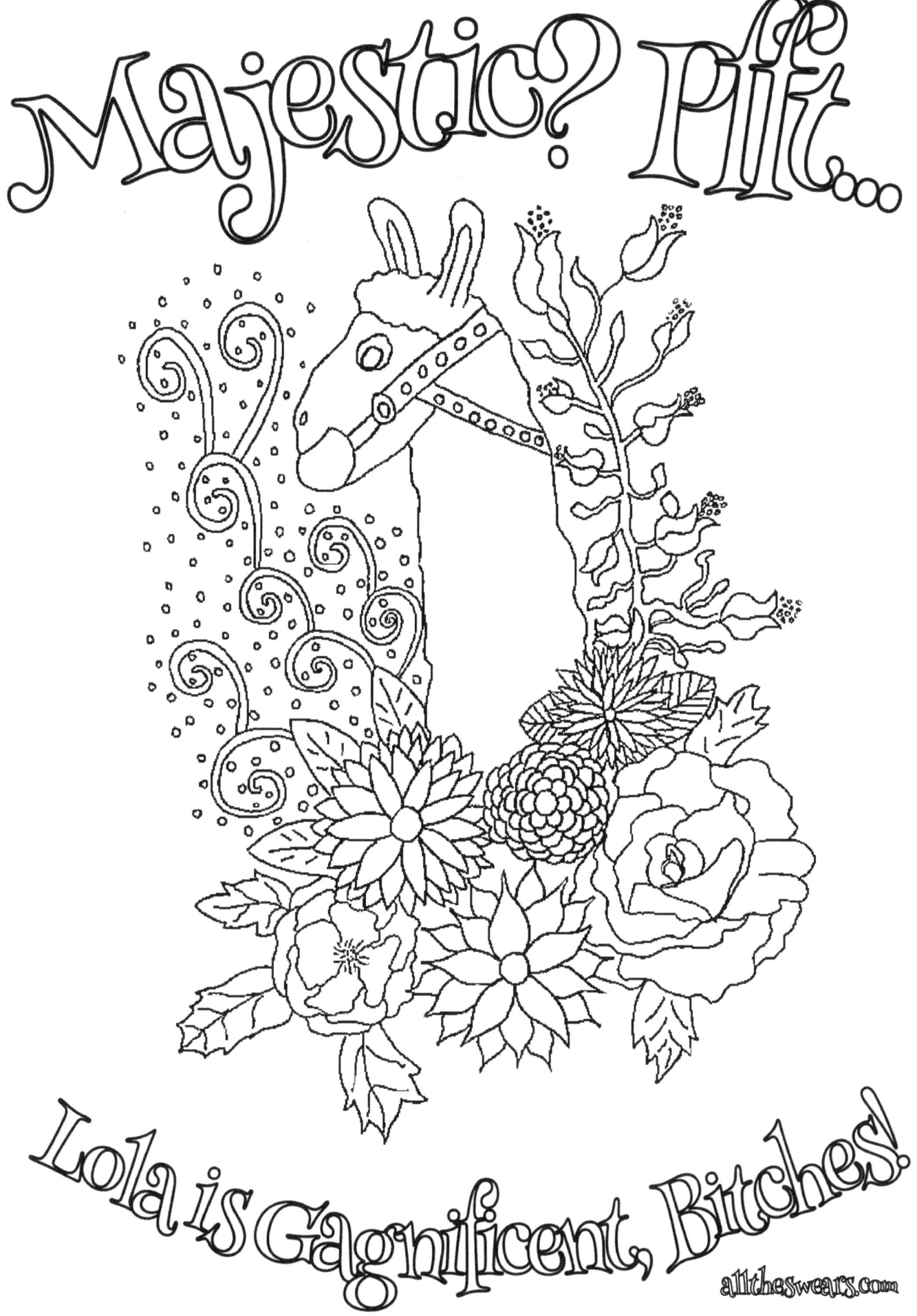

allthesswears.com

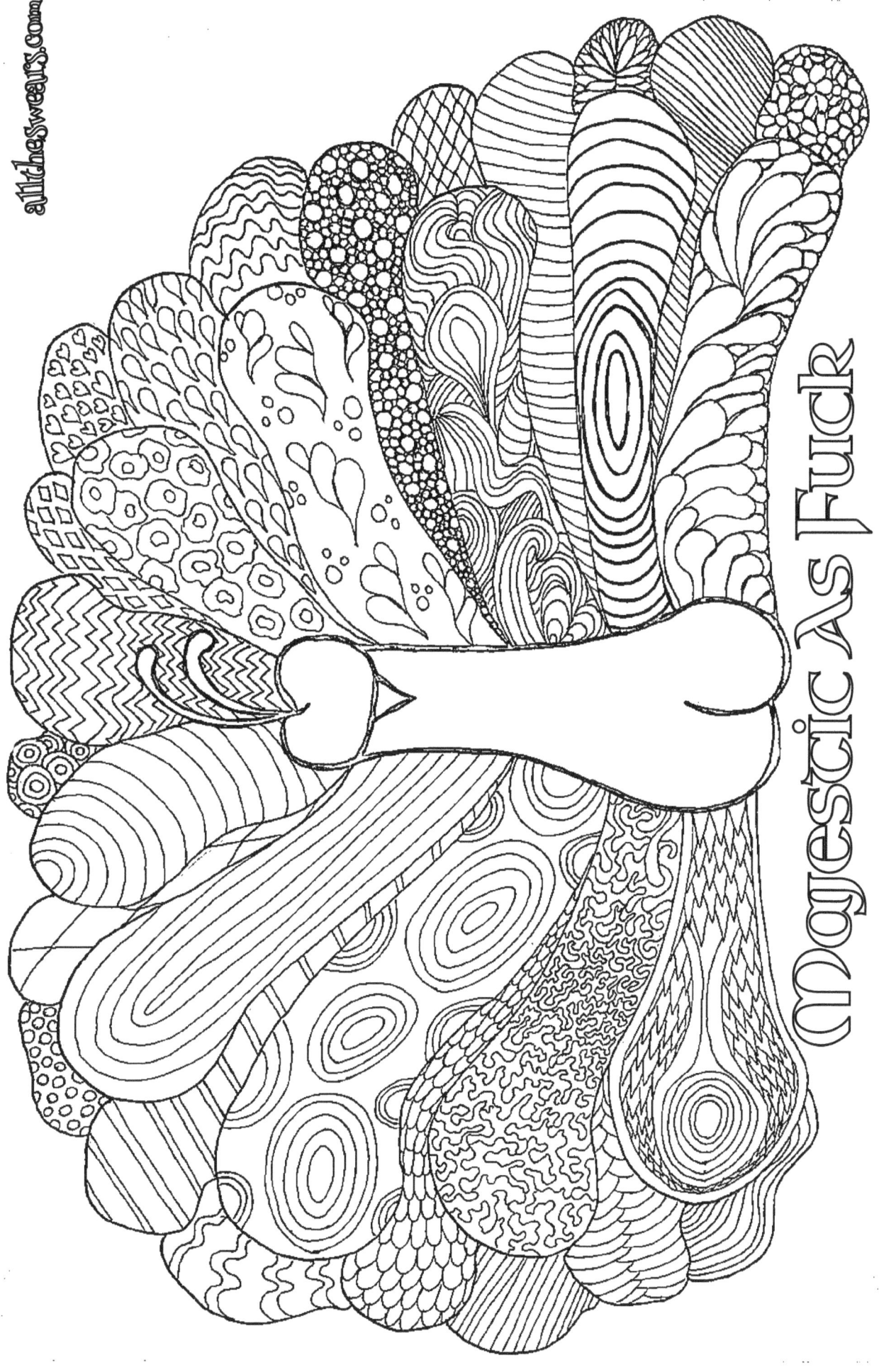

Majestic As Fuck

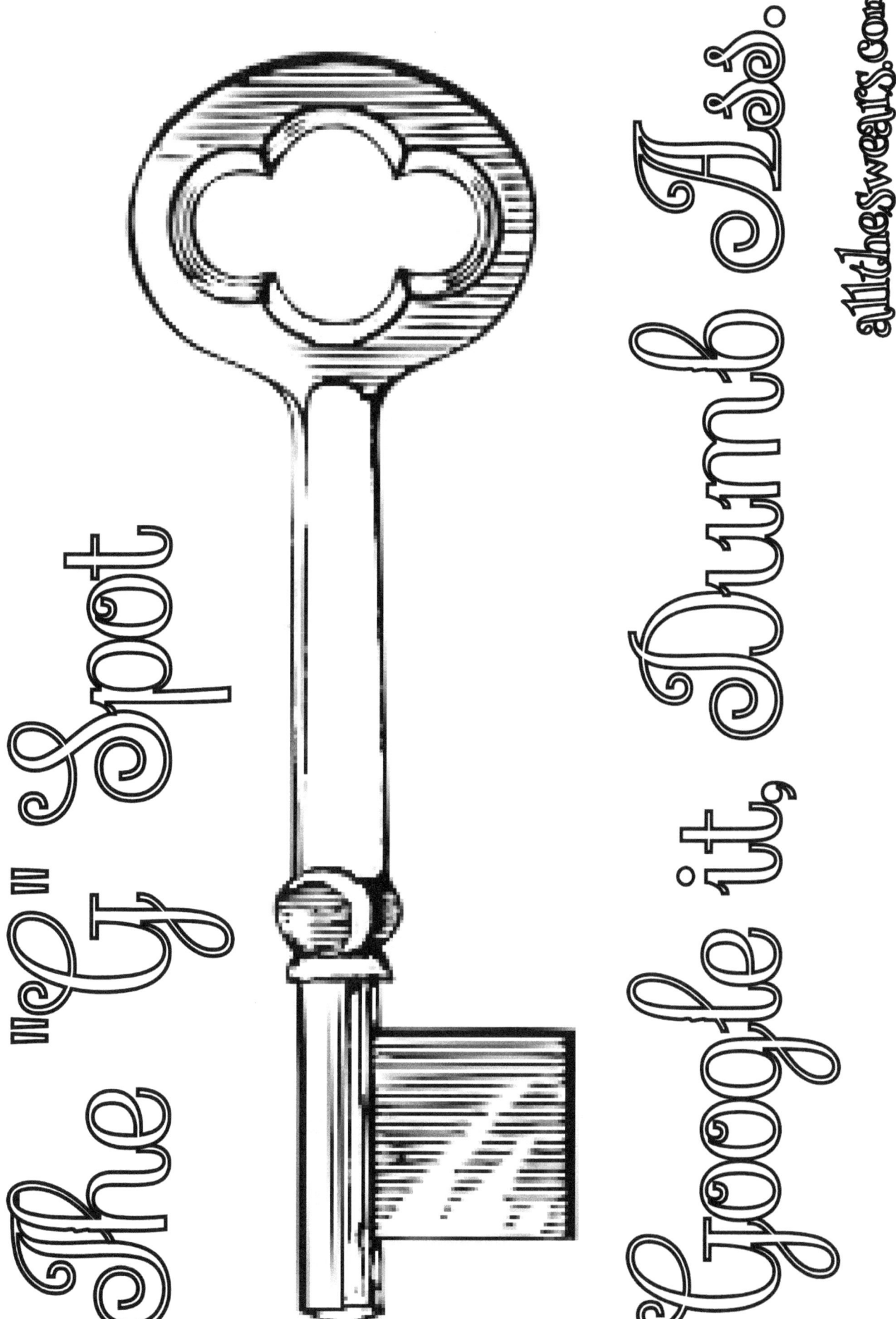

The "G" Spot

Google it, Dumb Ass.

Shenanigans

Because

Life Is More Fun

When you are

Up To Something

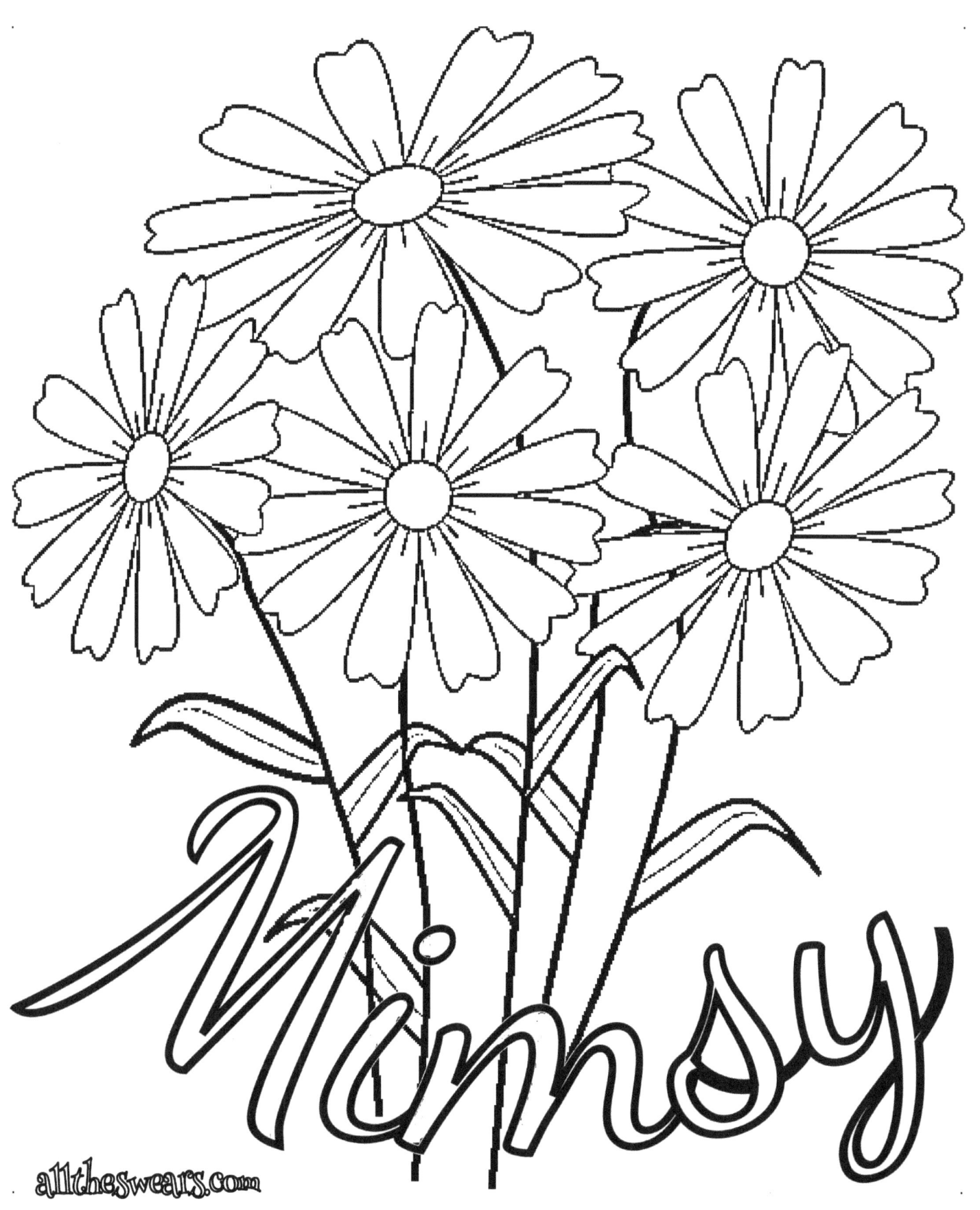

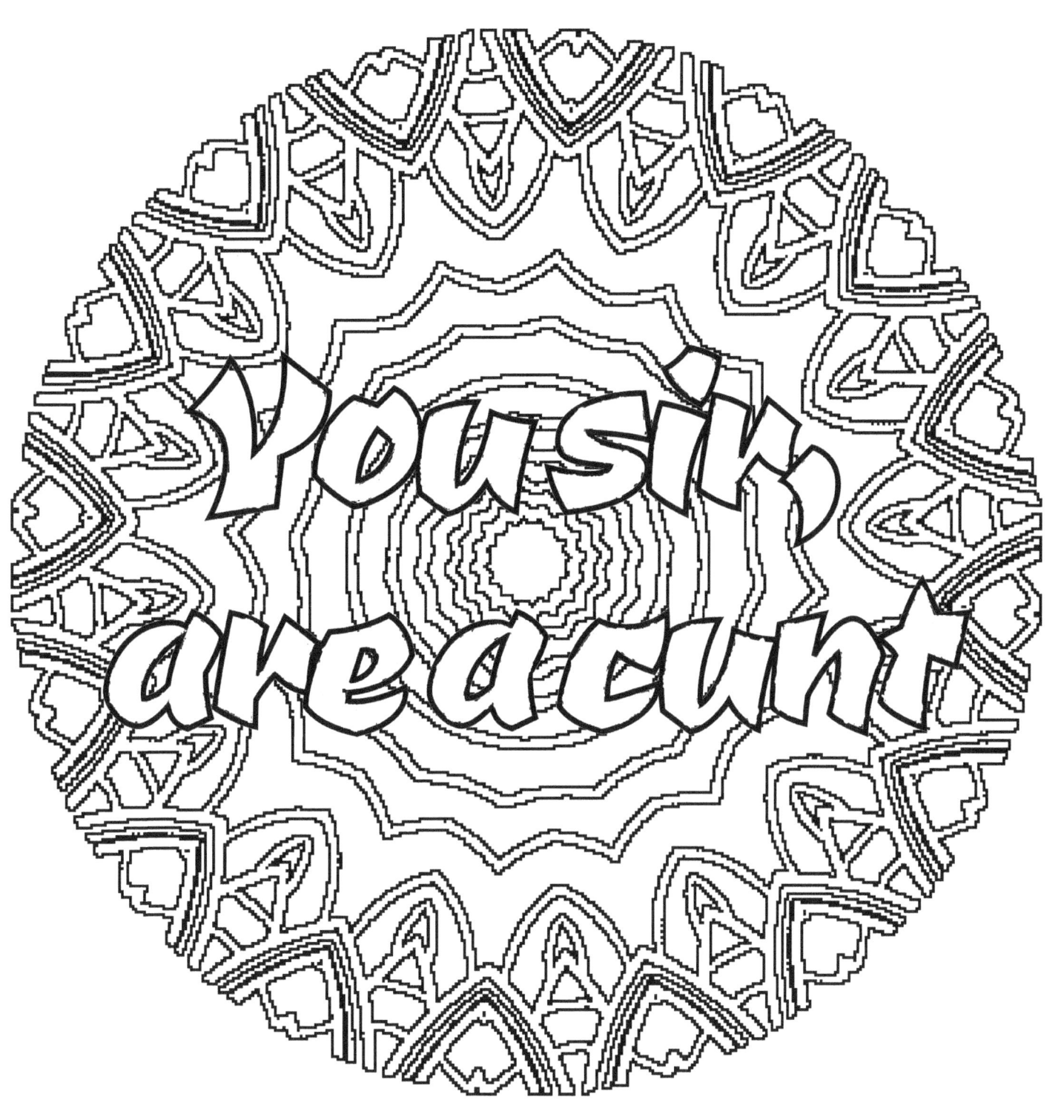

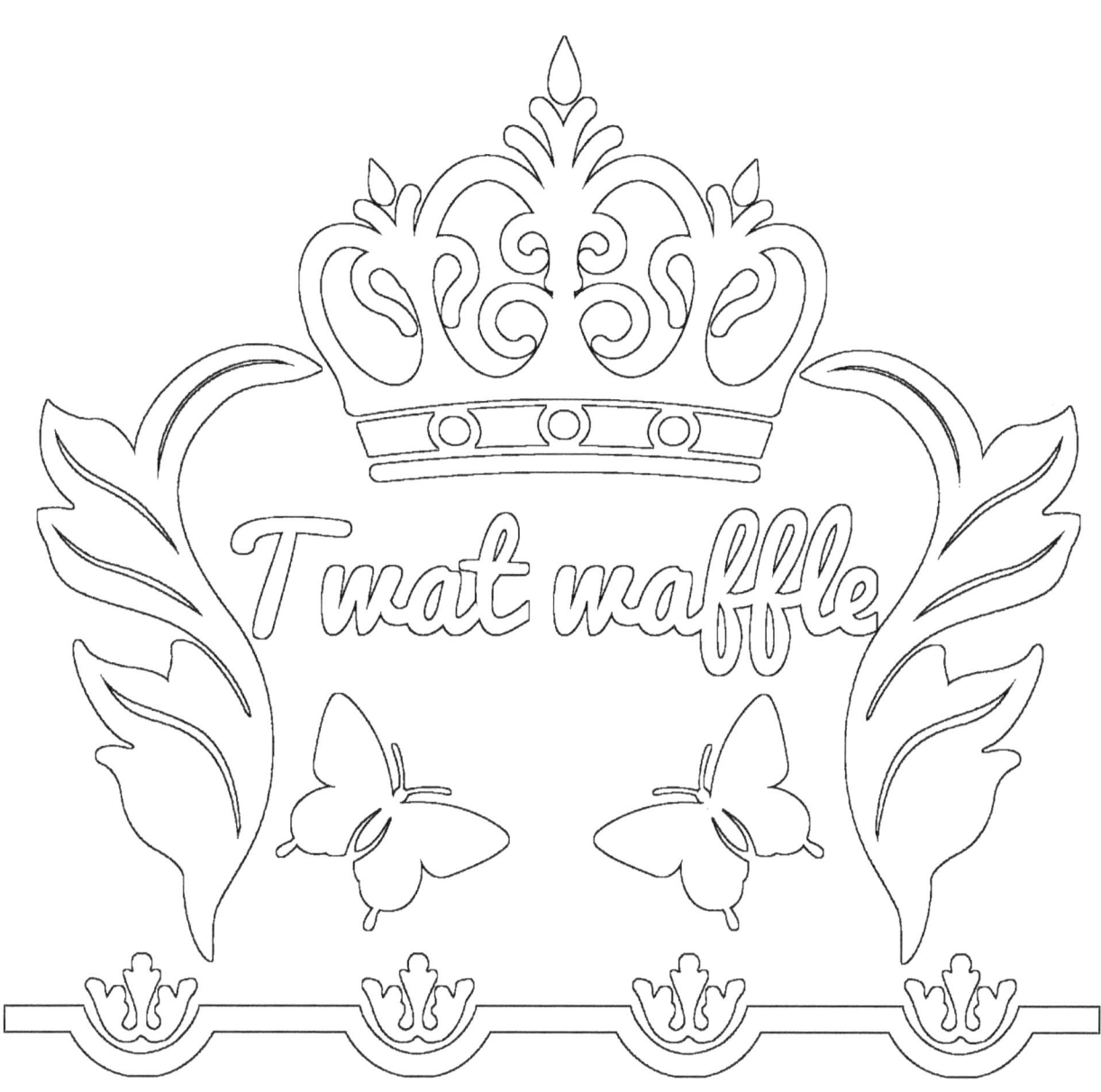

allthesWears.com

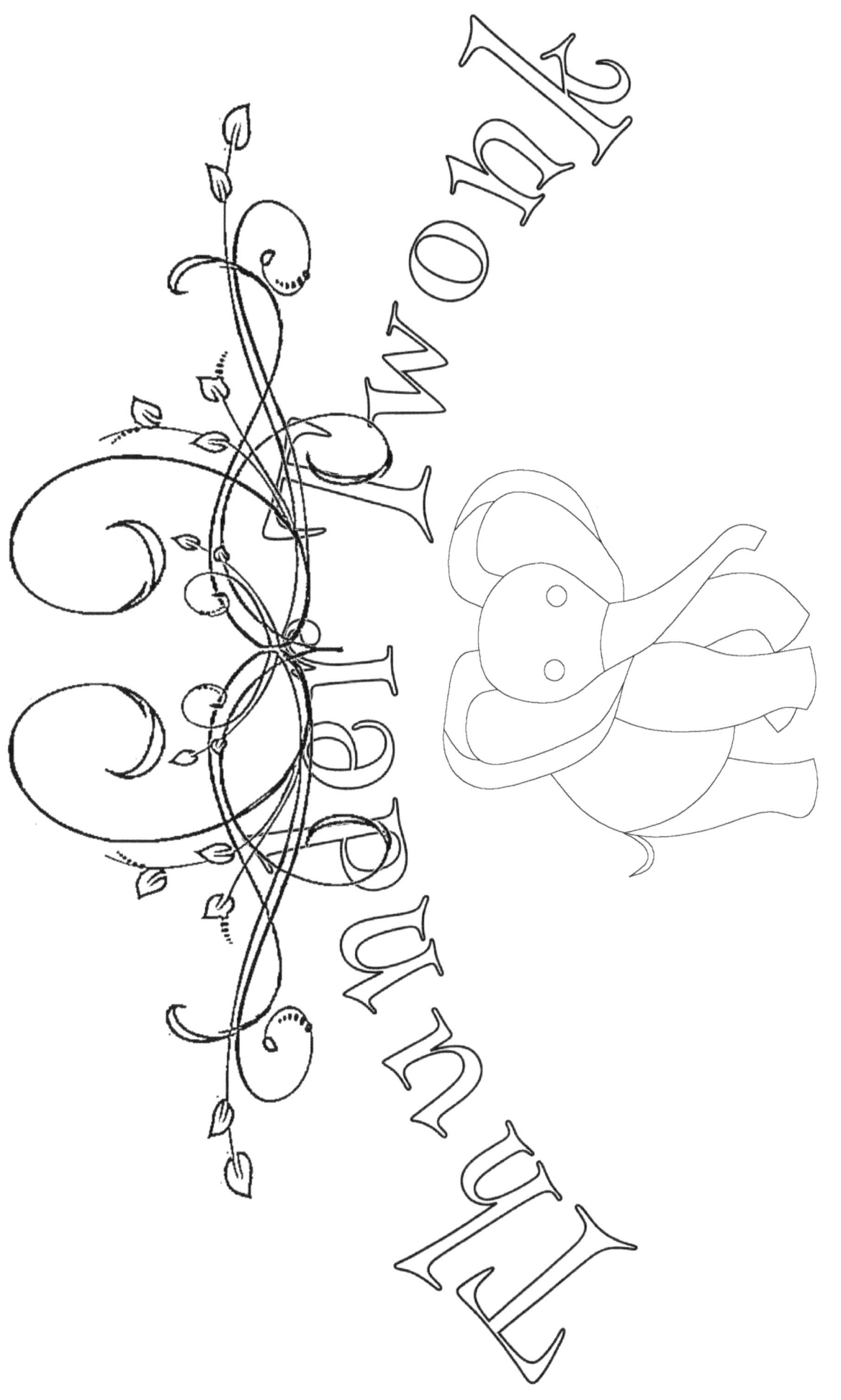

Vagina

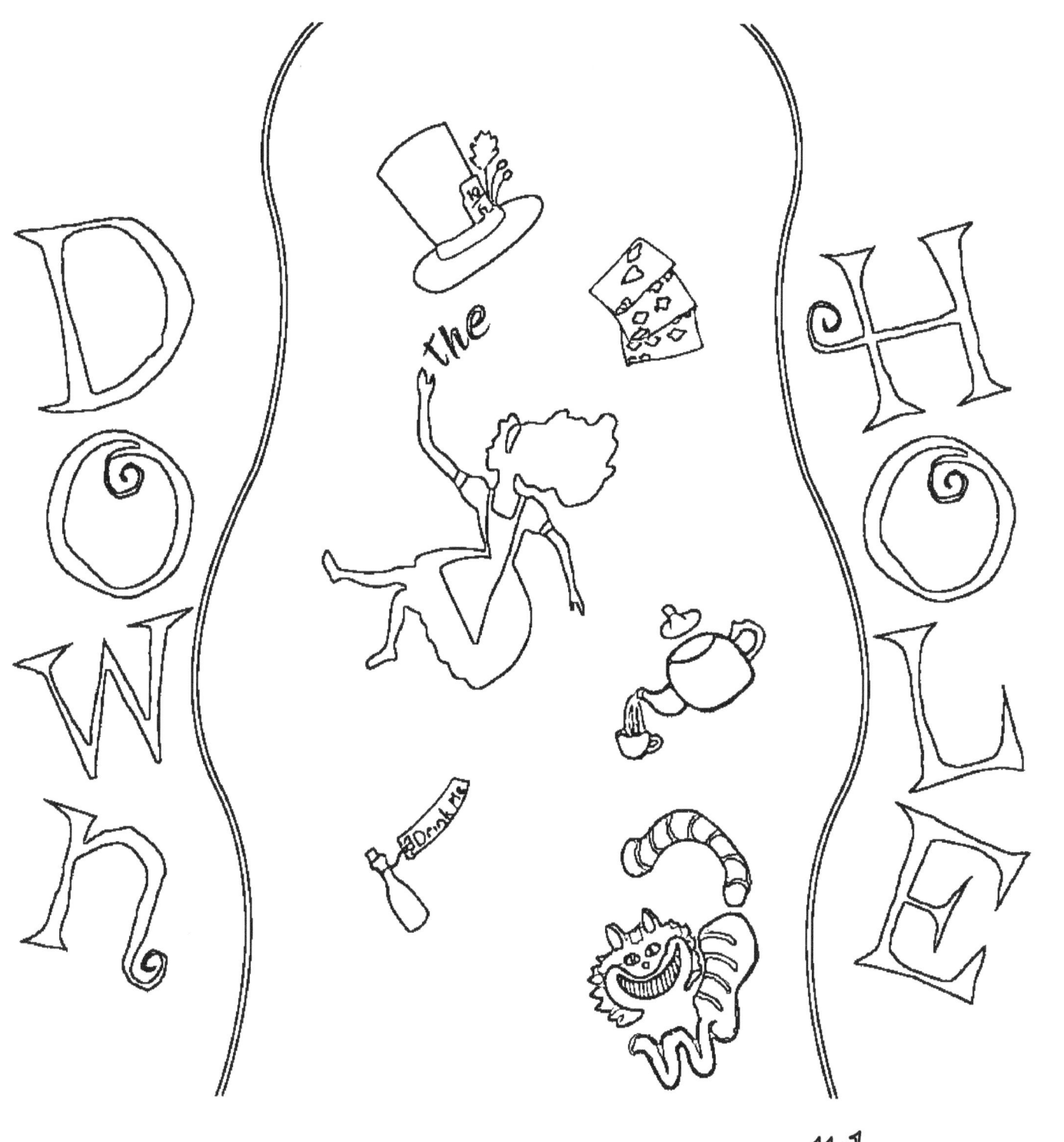

DOWN the HOLE

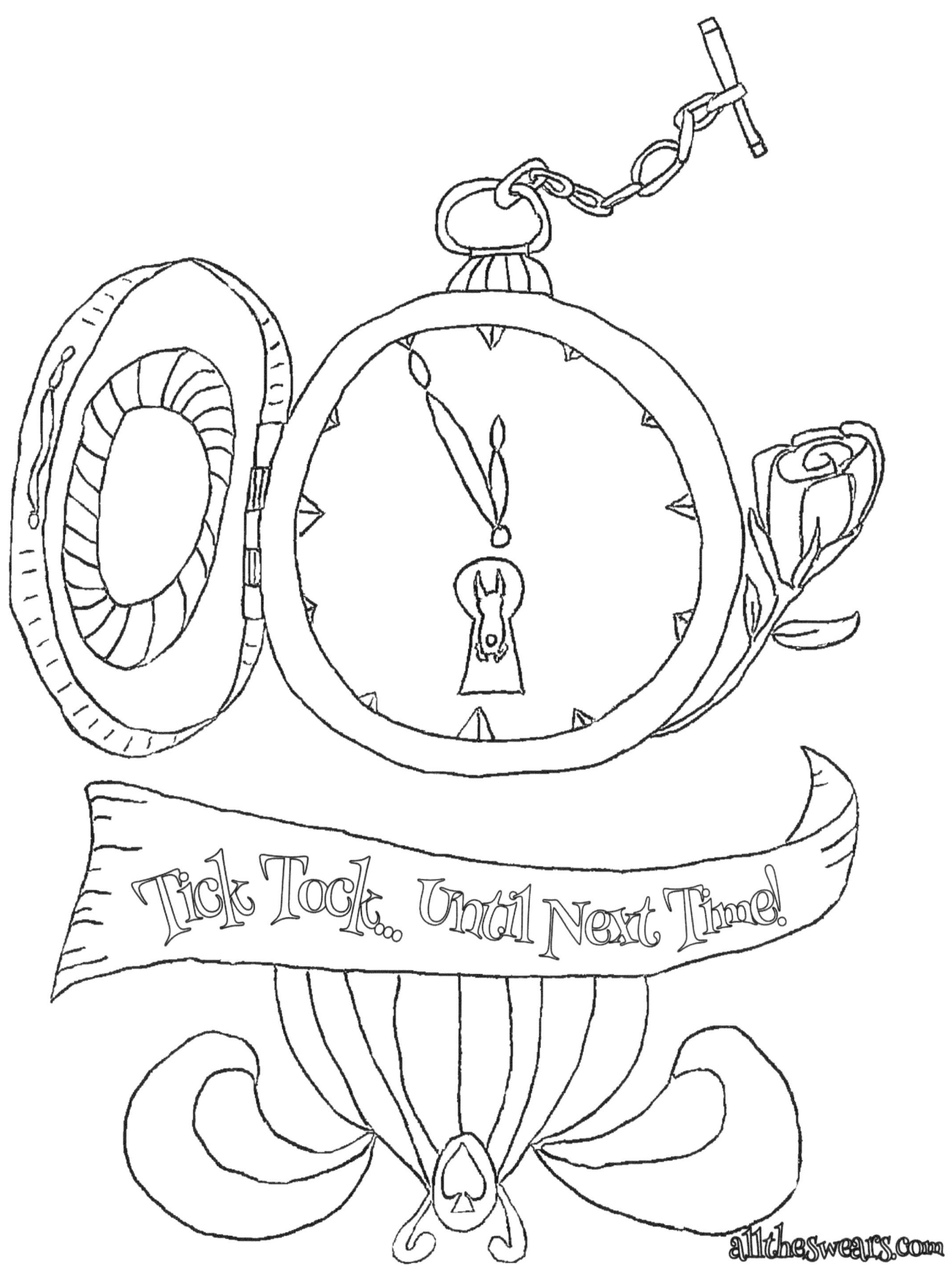

Tick Tock... Until Next Time!

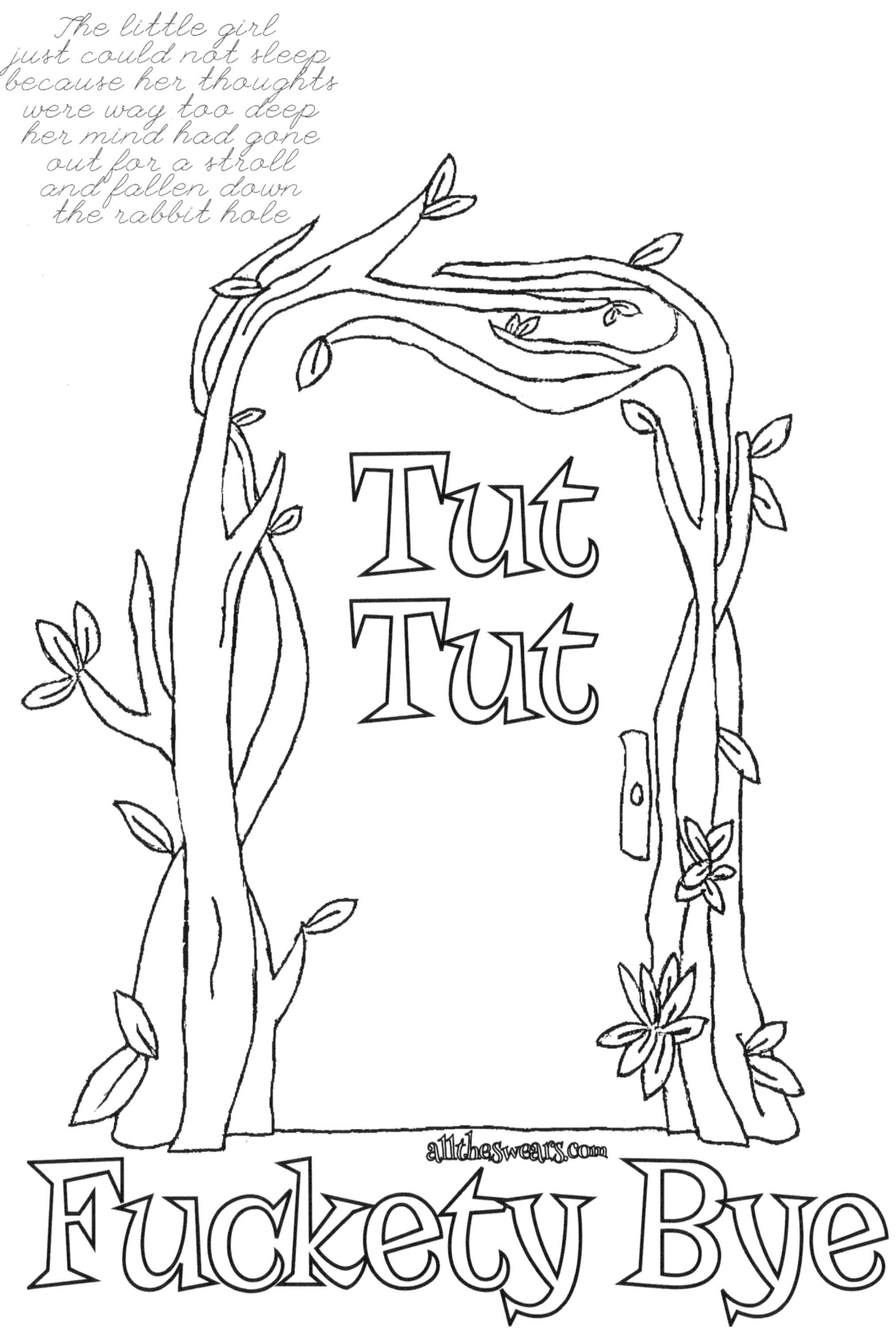

The little girl
just could not sleep
because her thoughts
were way too deep
her mind had gone
out for a stroll
and fallen down
the rabbit hole

Tut Tut

Fuckety Bye

About The Authors

Scarlet Hayes is a recovering lawyer. After receiving one too many propositions for inmate boyfriends, Scarlet decided that her time might be better spent making people laugh on purpose, rather than by tripping over deputies as they lunge to taser her unruly clients. She currently owns Madcasm Publishing as well as Wonderland, LLC, her two media babies and her favorite endeavors. She occasionally uses her legal education for a real purpose too, and teaches various business and legal courses for bachelors and masters degree students, since those student loans don't pay for themselves, as the federal government keeps reminding her. Now, she just uses the taser as a threat to keep her minions in line, i.e., her fighter pilot husband, their two adorable children, and her menagerie of asshole animals.

You can follow Scarlet's many adventures on Facebook at facebook.com/downthehole, facebook.com/alltheswears, and facebook.com/Madcasm. You can follow her blog at dthinwonderland.com, though she rarely remembers to post a damn thing there because her ADD is about as shiny as a new squirrel. Madcasm.com is a bit better and is always accepting submissions from aspiring writers and bloggers. You can also look for a new website from alltheswears.com as soon as she figures out what in the hell she's doing, there.

She also likes short walks to the refrigerator for large glasses of wine. Cheers!

Amber Lite is a fulltime mommy, print manager, artist, and vulgar epithet connoisseur. She makes up for the resulting sleep deficit by mainlining obscene amounts of coffee.

As captain, crew, mess cook, and cruise director of MNWNW, LLC, she's got huge...coffee mugs and wine glasses, on which she paints obnoxious phrases and vulgar cartoons threatening to punch a person in the bitch wrinkle.

She also enjoys cooking and painting on canvas, but recommends that these activities not be engaged in simultaneously while drinking large amounts of wine, recalling the infamous jalapeno incident of 2016. These and other shenanigans can be followed on Facebook at facebook.com/mommyneedswinenotwhine and of course, at facebook.com/alltheswears.

Links and Shit

If you want to stalk AllTheSwears:

Our virtually nonexistent (as of now) website: www.allthesswears.com
Our Facebook page, where we actually do participate: facebook.com/allthesswears
Twitter: @allthesswears
Instagram: allthesswears
Email us at allthesswears@gmail.com

Down The Hole/Scarlet Hayes:

Facebook Page – follow it. It's where all the action is: facebook.com/downthehole
Website/Blog. Don't bother checking it. I rarely post here: dthinwonderland.com
Twitter: @down_hole
Instagram: dthinwonderland
Email me at dthscarlet@gmail.com

Mommy Needs Wine, Not Whine/MNWNW/Amber Lite:

Facebook Page: facebook.com/mommyneedswinenotwhine
Blog: www.mommyneedswinenotwhine.com
Website – it's where you'll find the cool mugs and wine glasses: mnwnw.com
Twitter: @sauvblancmom
Email me at sauvblancmom@gmail.com

Madcasm Publishing:

Facebook Page: facebook.com/madcasm
Website: madcasm.wordpress.com
Twitter: @madcasm
Email us at madcapublishing@gmail.com